IT'S SNOWING!
BY GAIL GIBBONS

Holiday House / New York

To Dennis Jones

Special thanks to Eric Evenson of
the National Weather Service
South Burlington, Vermont

Printed and Bound in March 2016 at Toppan Leefung,
Dongguan City, China.
www.holidayhouse.com
First Edition
5 7 9 10 8 6 4

Library of Congress Cataloging-in-Publication Data
Gibbons, Gail.
It's snowing! / by Gail Gibbons. — 1st ed.
p. cm.
ISBN 978-0-8234-2237-1 (hardcover)
1. Snowflakes—Juvenile literature. 2. Snow—Juvenile literature. I. Title.
QC926.37.G53 2011
551.57'84—dc22
2010029570
ISBN 978-0-8234-2545-7 (paperback)

Small, soft flakes fall quietly from above. It's snowing!

It is cold, and winter clouds fill the sky.

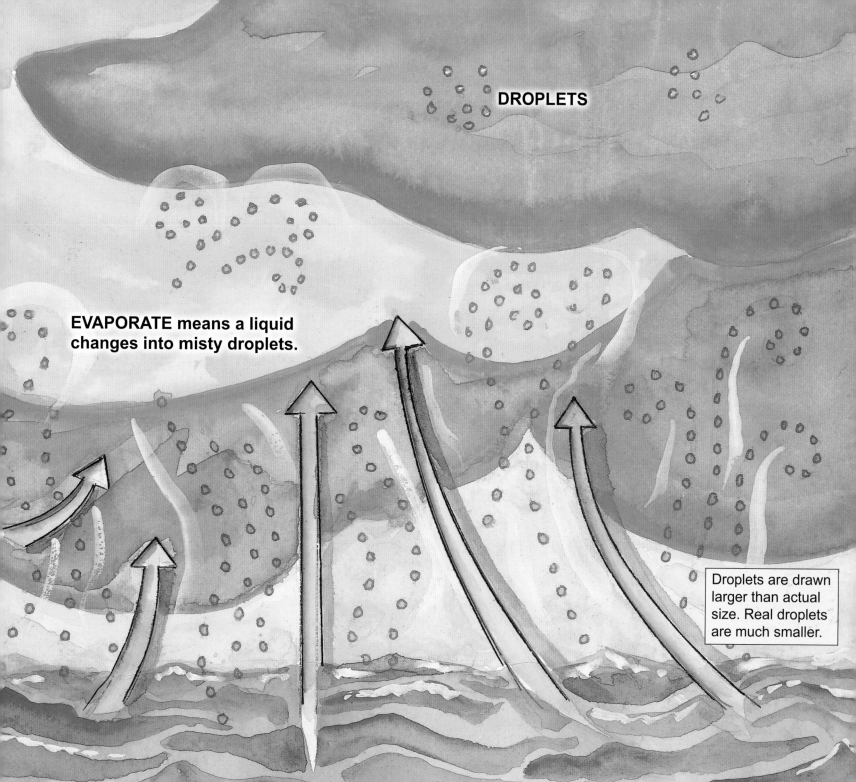

DROPLETS

EVAPORATE means a liquid changes into misty droplets.

Droplets are drawn larger than actual size. Real droplets are much smaller.

Clouds form when water evaporates from rivers, lakes, and oceans and then rises and cools. Clouds are made up of billions and billions of droplets of water floating in the air.

5

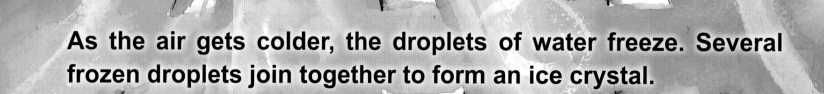

ICE CRYSTALS

As the air gets colder, the droplets of water freeze. Several frozen droplets join together to form an ice crystal.

SOME DIFFERENT ICE CRYSTALS

As ICE CRYSTALS form, they may look like needles, columns, flat plates, and many other shapes and designs.

Ice crystals are drawn larger than actual size. Real ice crystals are much smaller.

Ice crystals come in many shapes and designs.

Ice crystals of all shapes and sizes float into one another and join together to create a snowflake.

Snowflakes form when cloud
temperatures are below freezing,
32° Fahrenheit (0° Celsius).

Soon more and more ice crystals attach themselves, making
the snowflake larger.

When snowflakes get large and heavy enough, they fall from the clouds. It's snowing!

SOME DIFFERENT SNOWFLAKES

Scientists believe that no two snowflakes look exactly alike. Each one appears to be different in design, shape, and size from all other snowflakes.

Snowflakes almost always have either six sides or six points.

SNOW FALLS ON ALL SEVEN CONTINENTS

Snow most often falls in places where winters are cold, but it can snow in places where winters are usually warm.

EUROPE

Helsinki, Finland, is the snowiest city in Europe. It has an average of 101 days of snow per year.

It can be bitterly cold and snowy in the Gobi (GO-bee) Desert.

AFRICA

In Tanzania (tan-zuh-NEE-uh) there is always snow or ice on the top of Mount Kilimanjaro (ki-luh-mun-JAR-oh), which is within sight of the equator.

AUSTRALIA

There is skiing in the Snowy Mountains Australia.

14

SOUTH AMERICA

ANTARCTICA

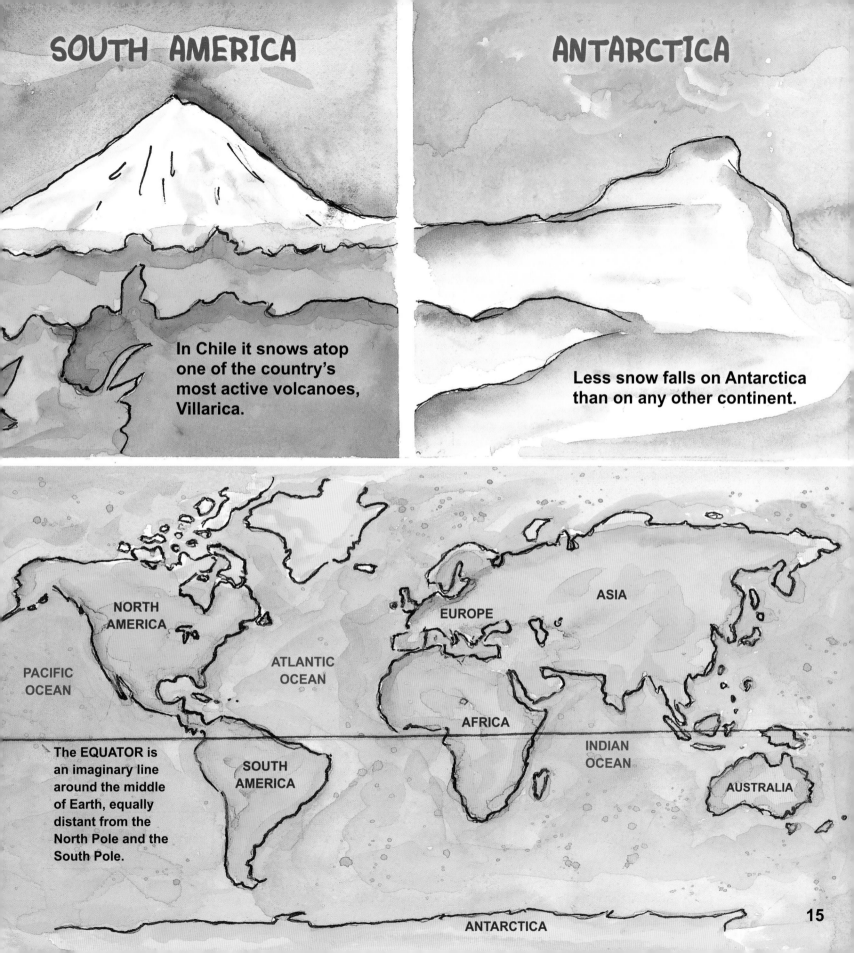

In Chile it snows atop one of the country's most active volcanoes, Villarica.

Less snow falls on Antarctica than on any other continent.

NORTH AMERICA

EUROPE

ASIA

PACIFIC OCEAN

ATLANTIC OCEAN

AFRICA

INDIAN OCEAN

AUSTRALIA

SOUTH AMERICA

The EQUATOR is an imaginary line around the middle of Earth, equally distant from the North Pole and the South Pole.

ANTARCTICA

SNOW FALLS TO THE GROUND IN DIFFERENT WAYS.

We say that it's snowing when there is a steady snowfall.

SNOW FLURRIES

There are snow flurries when it snows lightly and for short periods of time. Snow flurries can start and stop, and then start and stop again.

17

It is sleeting when snowflakes partially melt as they fall and then freeze again before they hit the ground. Sleet can be dangerous. It can be slippery outside.

SNOWSTORM

There is a snowstorm when a lot of snow falls. It may be windy. It can snow for hours, it can even snow for days. Snow covers the ground.

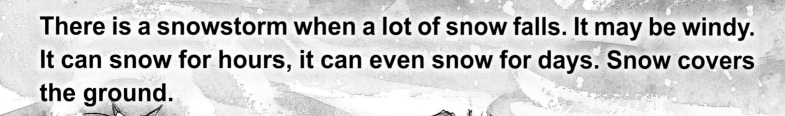

BLIZZARD

When falling snow and snow on the ground are blown by strong winds, SNOWDRIFTS are formed. Snowdrifts are large piles of snow that form along roads, up against buildings, and in many other places.

A blizzard happens when lots and lots of snow falls. The wind is howling. The snow is drifting. There can be whiteouts.

A WHITEOUT occurs when there is a heavy snowfall with strong winds. It is very hard to see.

Blizzards can be dangerous.

SNOW DAY!

METEOROLOGISTS are scientists who study weather.

Meteorologists often warn about dangerous conditions when a snowstorm or blizzard is approaching.

A WINTER STORM WATCH means that a storm may be coming to your area in 12 to 36 hours. How severe the storm may be is uncertain.

A WINTER STORM WARNING means that your area can receive heavy snow within the next 24 hours.

A BLIZZARD WARNING means that heavy snow, strong winds, and whiteout conditions are coming. Snowdrifts can be high, and the temperature will be low.

People are told to stay at home. Schools and businesses may close.

Sometimes on busy city streets machines called payloaders lift snow and drop it into dump trucks that haul the snow away.

The weight of snow or ice can bring down tree limbs and power lines, and cause other damage. Cleanup crews get to work.

After big storms there is a lot of work to be done. Snowplows push snow off the roads and highways. Walkways are shoveled.

SNOW CAN BE FUN!

People bundle up to stay warm and dry when they go outside.
Kids build snowmen and snow forts.

SWISH! Some people go skiing and snowboarding. Sleds and toboggans slide down hillsides.

SNOWSHOES help you walk on the surface of deep snow.

Some children make snow angels. Others take long walks in the quiet countryside. It is beautiful and peaceful all around.

Snow can be helpful in many ways. It acts like a huge blanket that protects plants and wildlife. As the snow melts, water trickles into rivers and streams. It also seeps into the ground where plants will grow when warmer weather returns.

Look all around. The snow is beautiful!

HOW TO STAY WARM OUTSIDE

HAT

SCARF

LAYERS OF LIGHT- WEIGHT CLOTHING

COAT

SOMETIMES EARMUFFS

JACKET

GLOVES

JACKET WITH HOOD

MITTENS

SOME CHILDREN WEAR SNOWSUITS.

BOOTS

BE PREPARED IF A SNOWSTORM IS COMING.

CHECKLISTS

FRESH WATER
SPARE BATTERIES
FIRST-AID KIT
NONPERISHABLE FOODS
FLASHLIGHT
BATTERY-POWERED RADIO
SHOVELS

MAKE SURE YOU ARE IN A SAFE PLACE WITH AN ADULT.

BRING YOUR PETS INSIDE.

LISTEN TO WEATHER FORECASTERS TO BE ON THE ALERT.

WATER

BATTERIES

CAN FO

SEE SNOWFLAKES CLOSE UP.

Go outside when the snow is falling gently.

Bring a piece of black paper with you.

Hold it out flat toward the sky.

Snowflakes will land on the paper's surface.

You can study snowflakes closer by looking through a magnifying glass.

Look very carefully and you will see many snowflake patterns.

It's believed Wilson Bentley was the first person to take pictures of snowflakes. He used a camera that magnified them. In 1928, he took more than 100 photographs in Vermont where he lived. He became known as Snowflake Bentley.

When the temperature goes above the freezing mark of 32° Fahrenheit (0° Celsius), snow that has fallen begins to melt. When the temperature drops below the freezing mark again, it turns to ice.

The largest snowflake ever recorded was in the state of Montana. It was 15 inches (38 centimeters) wide.

Perhaps the most famous blizzard in the United States took place from March 11 to March 14 in 1888. It is called the Great Blizzard of 1888. Almost 50 inches (1.3 meters) of snow fell along the East Coast, from Massachusetts to New Jersey. Winds blew more than 45 miles per hour (72.4 kilometers per hour). Some snowdrifts were as high as 50 feet (15.2 meters). Everyday activity came to a halt for almost a week.

The biggest snowfall in one day happened in Silver Lake, Colorado, on April 14, 1921. The snow was 6 feet 4 inches (1.9 meters) deep.

RAIN   SNOW

A rainstorm may result in 1 inch (2.5 centimeters) of rain. If it had snowed instead, there would have been about 10 inches (25 centimeters) of snow.

An avalanche is when a mass snow suddenly slides down th side of a mountain, destroying everything in its path.

WEBSITES
UNITED STATES
www.nws.noaa.gov
CANADA
www.weatheroffice.gc.ca/canada_e.html